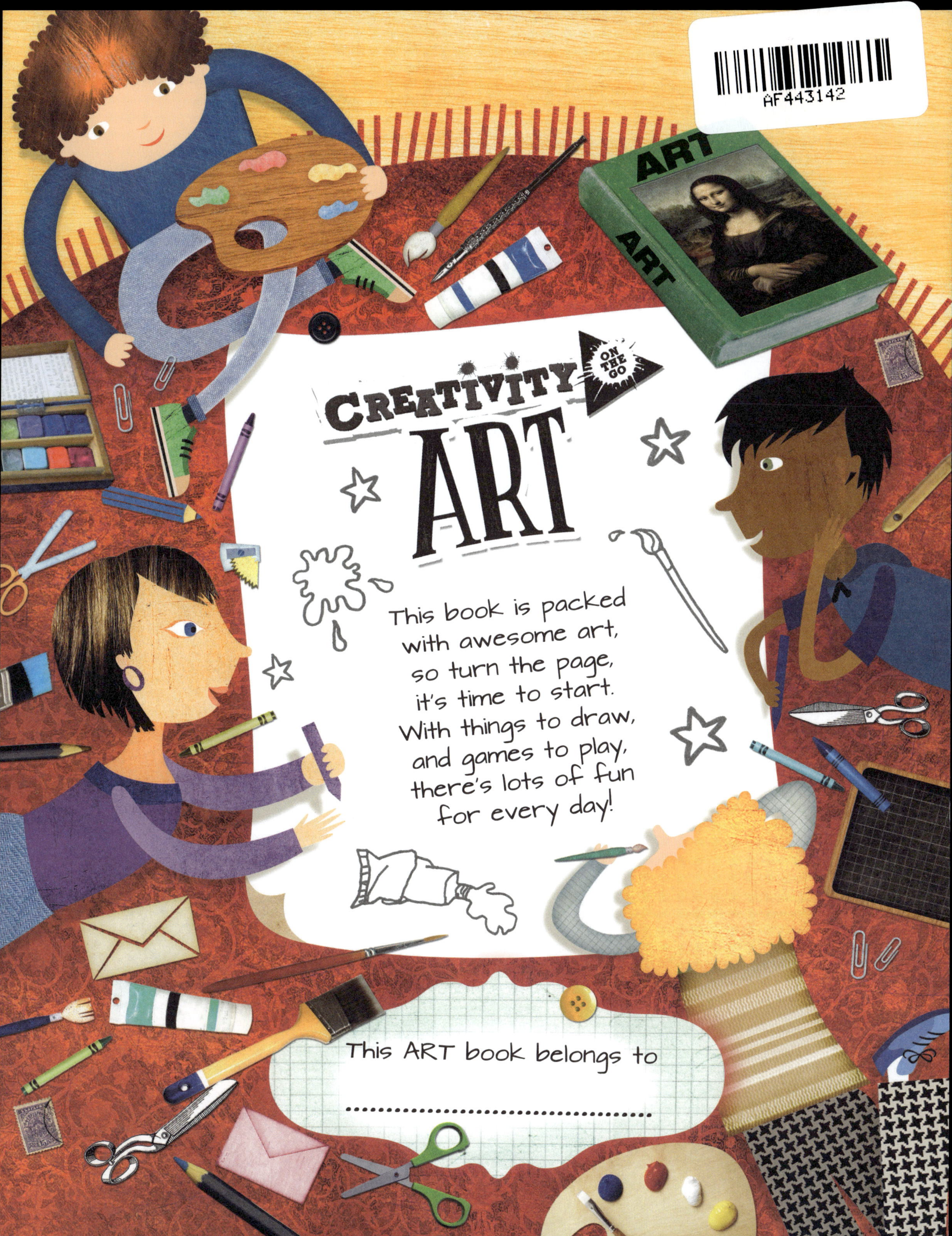
AF443142
ART
ART
CREATIVITY ON THE GO
ART
This book is packed
with awesome art,
so turn the page,
it's time to start.
With things to draw,
and games to play,
there's lots of fun
for every day!
This ART book belongs to

What's inside this book?

Wonderful art!

This book is packed with art and famous artists, such as Vincent Van Gogh and Leonardo da Vinci. Follow in their artistic footsteps as you draw, paint and colour!

Things to make

Make a collage on page 15, a fancy frame for your artwork on page 25, a door hanger on page 53 or an artistic mask on page 61. There's colourful pull-out art paper to get creative with too!

Stickers

Your arty stickers are at the back of the book. Use them on the sticker scenes or anywhere you like!

Stencils

Look for the stencils inside (hint - go to the back of the book). Then hunt for the pages where you can use them.

Puzzles and Games

There are dot-to-dots, mazes, spot the differences and games. Race to finish a masterpiece on page 16 or match up the artists on page 71.

A catalogue record for this book is available from the British Library.
10 9 8 7 6 5 4 3 2 1
ISBN: 978 1 78312 212 7
Printed and bound in China

Author: Ruth Thomson
Executive editor: Paul Virr
Senior art editor: Jake da'Costa
Design: Zoë Dissell
Illustrations: Agnese Baruzzi & Elle Ward
Production: Claire Halligan

With thanks to Beatrice and Mila for being such wonderful art critics.

Picture Credits:

The publishers thank the following sources for their kind permission to reproduce the pictures in this book: Pg 8: Henri Rousseau, *Surprised.* The Bridgeman Art Library/National Gallery, London, UK; Pg 20: Giuseppe Arcimboldo, *Basket of Fruit.* Private Collection; Pg 24: Rodin, *The Thinker.* www.istockphoto.com; Pg 28: Leonardo da Vinci *The Mona Lisa.* The Bridgeman Art Library/Louvre, Paris, France; Pg 30: Albrecht Dürer, *Indian Rhinoceros.* www.istockphoto.com; Pgs 36-37: Vincent Van Gogh, *Bedroom in Arles.* The Bridgeman Art Library/The Art Institute of Chicago, IL, USA; Pg 40: Pieter Bruegel, *Children's Games.* The Bridgeman Art Library/Kunsthistorisches Museum, Vienna, Austria; Pg 4: Paul Klee, *Castle and Sun.* The Bridgeman Art Library/Private Collection; Pg 48: Gustav Klimt, *Tree of Life.* Akg-Images/Erich Lessing; Pg 53: Michelangelo Buonarroti, *David.* www.istockphoto.com; Pg 56: Ando Hiroshige, *Stormy Sea at the Naruto Rapids.* The Bridgeman Art Library/Blackburn Museum and Art Gallery, Lancashire, UK. Pg 66: *Statue of Peter the Great.* www.istockphoto.com

Calling all artists!

Are you a budding artist? Answer these questions to find out!

ART TEST   Tick all that apply to you. ✓

1. I like to use my imagination.

2. If I see a piece of paper I just have to doodle!

3. I love messing about with pencils and paints.

4. My favourite colour changes every day.

5. I love looking at things in museums or galleries.

If you ticked most of the boxes, you are an ARTIST. Get creative now!

Finishing touches

Complete the pictures in this gallery.

SELF-PORTRAIT

Me, by myself,
the artist!

STILL LIFE

Colourful flowers
in a vase.

STORY PICTURE

A princess is rescued from a sea monster!

These labels describe the different types of picture that artists paint.

LANDSCAPE

A lovely view of green hills and trees.

PORTRAIT

ABSTRACT

His majesty, the King!

A colourful pattern of lines and shapes.

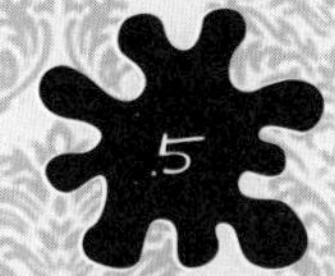

How to draw a face

Copy each step-by-step drawing into the box below it.

Draw an oval face shape and two ears. Add faint guidelines.

Draw eyebrows in line with the top of the ears. Add eyes below.

A great start!

Looking good!

Add a nose. Make sure it's level with the bottom of the ears.

Lastly, draw in a smiling or a sad mouth and add some hair!

Nearly there!

Another MASTERPIECE!

surprised!
What animal is hiding in this jungle picture?

HENRI ROUSSEAU 1844 - 1910
FRENCH PAINTER

ROUSSEAU PAINTED SURPRISED! WITHOUT EVER SEEING A JUNGLE. HE USED THE BOTANICAL GARDENS OF PARIS AND STUFFED WILD ANIMALS FOR INSPIRATION.

Colour in the shapes to reveal another animal hidden in the jungle.
Colour the shapes with a cross brown.
Colour the other shapes in many shades of green.
The answer is on page 80.
9

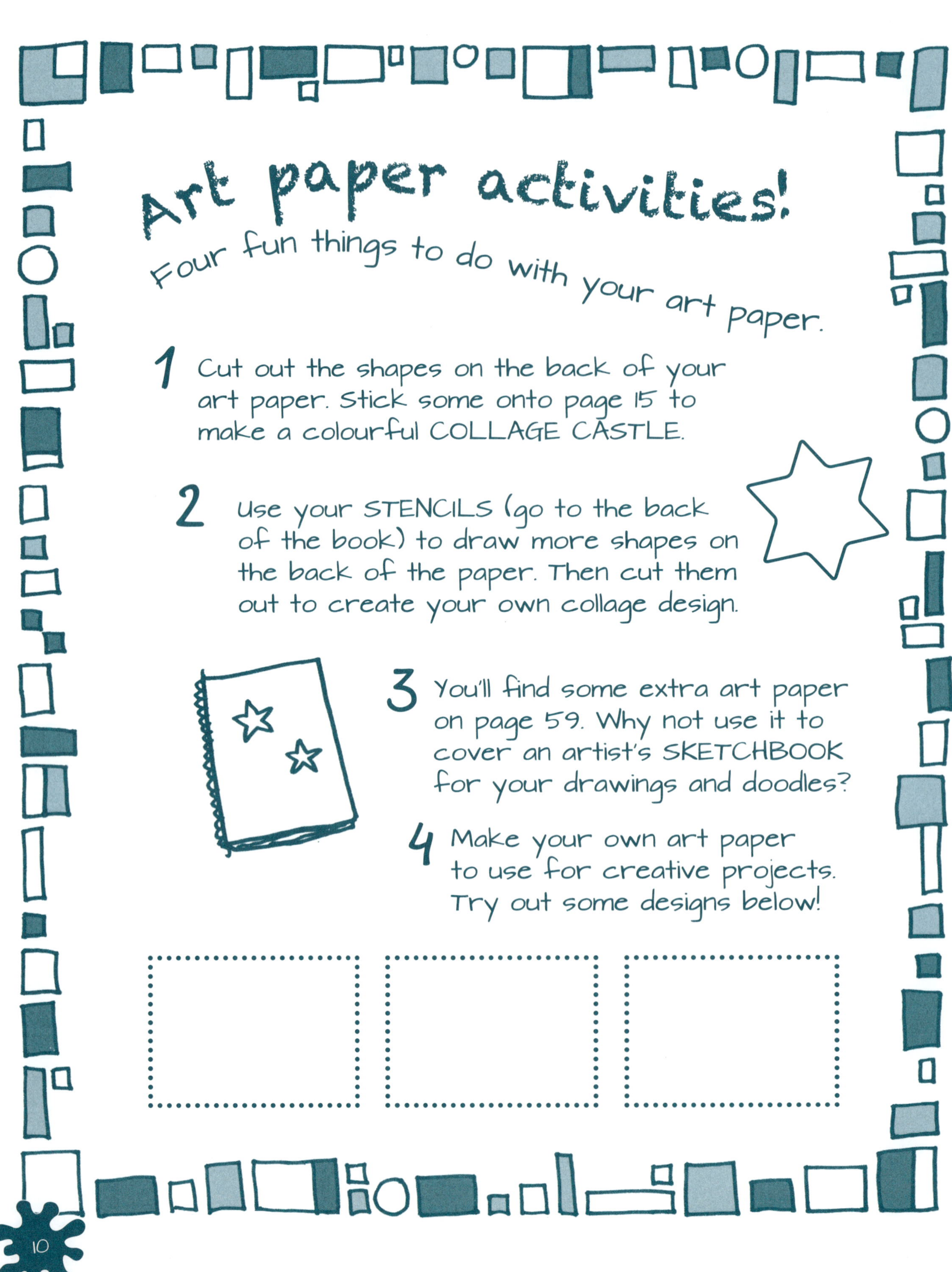

Art paper activities!

Four fun things to do with your art paper.

1 Cut out the shapes on the back of your art paper. Stick some onto page 15 to make a colourful COLLAGE CASTLE.

2 Use your STENCILS (go to the back of the book) to draw more shapes on the back of the paper. Then cut them out to create your own collage design.

3 You'll find some extra art paper on page 59. Why not use it to cover an artist's SKETCHBOOK for your drawings and doodles?

4 Make your own art paper to use for creative projects. Try out some designs below!

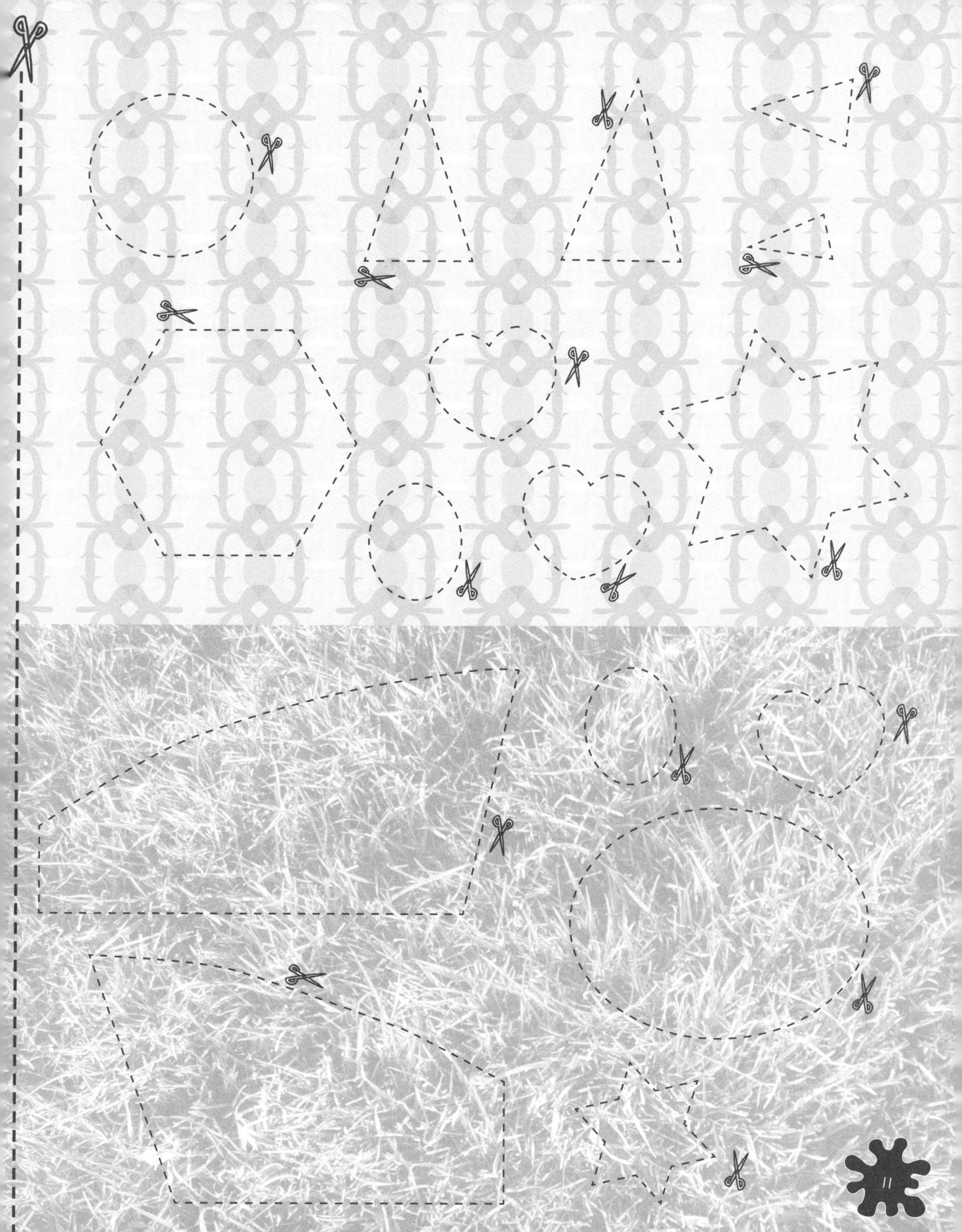

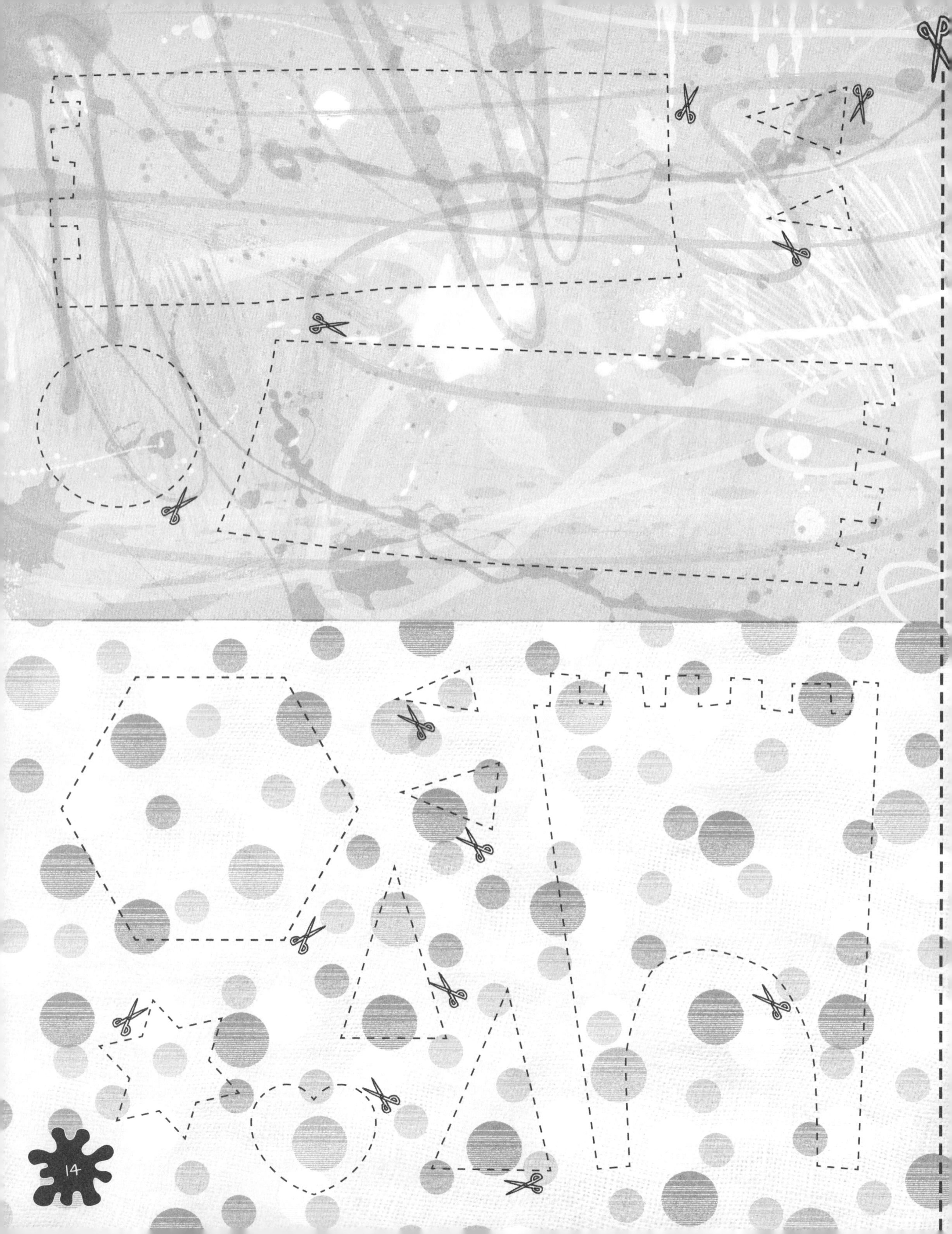

Collage castle

Give this castle an artistic new look!

Stick the cut-out shapes from your art paper onto the castle.

Art Show Scramble

Are you quick on the draw? Race to finish a picture for the Art Show!

HOW TO PLAY

1. This is a game for two or more players.
2. Each player needs a counter. Put it on the start.
3. Take turns to roll the dice and move your counter along the board.
4. Follow the instructions on any space that you land.
5. The winner is the first to reach the finish.

ART GALLERY
The first to get here is the winning artist. Congratulations!
25 Missed the bus. Miss a turn.
26
27 FINISH
22 Oops! Paint on your beret! Miss a turn to clean it.
21 Time to frame your masterpiece. Move ahead five spaces.
20
19 Using stencils was a great idea. Move to 20.
12 Change of colour scheme! Go back three spaces.
13 Great brushwork! Move to 16.
14
11
15 Waiting for paint to dry! Miss a turn.
18 Dropped the paints! Go back four spaces.
10
16
17
17

A is for artist!

In the Middle Ages, monks wrote books by hand, adding pictures and decorated first letters.

Colour in this fancy letter. Add jewel stickers to make it look really precious.

To the studio!

The Bauhaus was a famous German school that taught art, architecture, craft and design.

Quick! Help this artist find her way to the studio before her painting dries!

The answer is on page 80.

19

Fruit faces

Is this really a fruit basket?
Turn the page upside-down.

ARCIMBOLDO PAINTED STRANGE PORTRAITS WITH OBJECTS SUCH AS FRUIT, VEGETABLES, FLOWERS AND EVEN FISH!

FRAGILE!

Or is it a funny face?

Create your own funny fruit face.
Turn the page to see what to do.
21

Make a fruit face

Here's what to do!

1 Ask an adult to help cut out the fruits (use the dotted lines on the other side of this page as a guide).

2 Arrange them into a face on a piece of paper. Try cherries for eyes, a pear for a chin, apples for cheeks and a banana for the mouth.

3 When you are happy with your face, stick the fruits down with glue.

4 Why not frame your picture? See the great picture frame you could make on pages 25 to 26!

22

Pretty palms

Draw around your hand, then follow the steps to decorate it.

1 Draw a pretty swirly pattern on the palm.

2 Give the fingertips a solid colour.

3 Use the same pattern for the fingers, thumb and wrist.

23

smart art
What on Earth is The Thinker wondering?

AUGUSTE RODIN 1840 - 1917
FRENCH SCULPTOR

THE THINKER IS MADE OF A HARD METAL CALLED BRONZE, SO IT CAN STAND OUTSIDE IN ALL KINDS OF WEATHER WITHOUT GETTING DAMAGED.

Maybe he can't decide what to wear? Draw him in a smart outfit here.

24

Frame it!
Make your own picture frame.

Turn the page to see how
to make your fancy picture
frame. Then use it to frame
one of your pictures!

How to make your picture frame

1 Carefully CUT this picture frame page out of your book.

2 GLUE the frame onto a piece of card (colour side face up).

3 When it's dry, ask a grown-up to help you CUT OUT the finished card frame, both inside and out.

4 Glue the frame over one of your pictures to make it a MASTERPIECE!

5 Don't forget to give your beautifully framed picture an artistic TITLE.

sound and vision!
Edvard Munch gave a picture the ear-splitting title: The Scream.
EDVARD MUNCH 1863 - 1944
NORWEGIAN PAINTER
It's far too noisy around here!
POW!
OUCH!
POP!
SSSSSSS!
SIZZLE!
What made these noises?
Draw a picture for each sound.

Mona Lisa makeover!

LEONARDO DA VINCI PAINTED MONA LISA WITH A MYSTERIOUS SMILE ON HER FACE.

Give Mona Lisa a new look. Use the hints below.

Cross

Amused

Scared

Embarrassed

THE FRENCH ARTIST MARCEL DUCHAMP DOODLED
A MOUSTACHE AND BEARD ON A POSTCARD OF THE
MONA LISA. IT BECAME HIS BEST-KNOWN ARTWORK!

pencil patterns

Albrecht Dürer never saw a real rhinoceros, so he used his imagination!

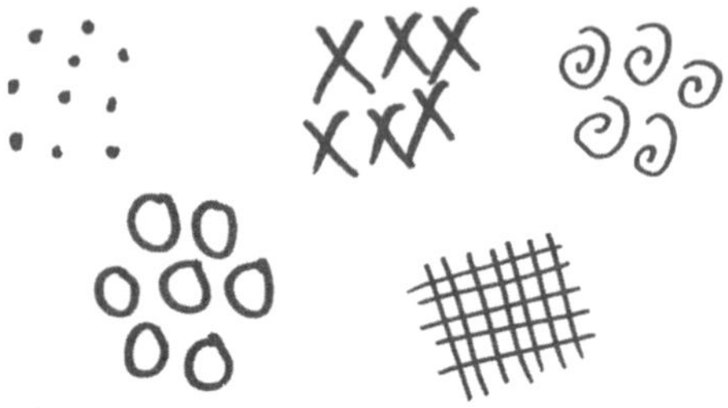

Draw a different pattern on each section of Dürer's rhino!

Try these patterns!

Amazing things to do with your stencils!

Turn to the back of the book to find your stencils. Tear them out of the book and get creative!

1 Use the stencils to create patterns for your own decorated designer STATIONERY, such as letters, birthday cards, envelopes and party invites.

2 Decorate a PICTURE FRAME, using your stencils to match a picture on a similar theme.

3 Make some patterned WRAPPING PAPER with your stencils - try the geometric shapes, the fruits and the animals.

4 Use your stencils to make a PICTURE that you can frame and give to a friend or a grown-up as a present.

A picnic picture
Grab your pencils and use your stencils to finish this picnic scene!
ART PARK
Grow some trees here.
Plant some flowers in the flowerbed.
Decorate the picnic rug!
32

Use some shapes
to make a kite.
What's the
weather like?
Add yourself!
What animal
is hiding?
What's in
the picnic
basket?
33

Computer art

Use stencil shapes to draw a robot.

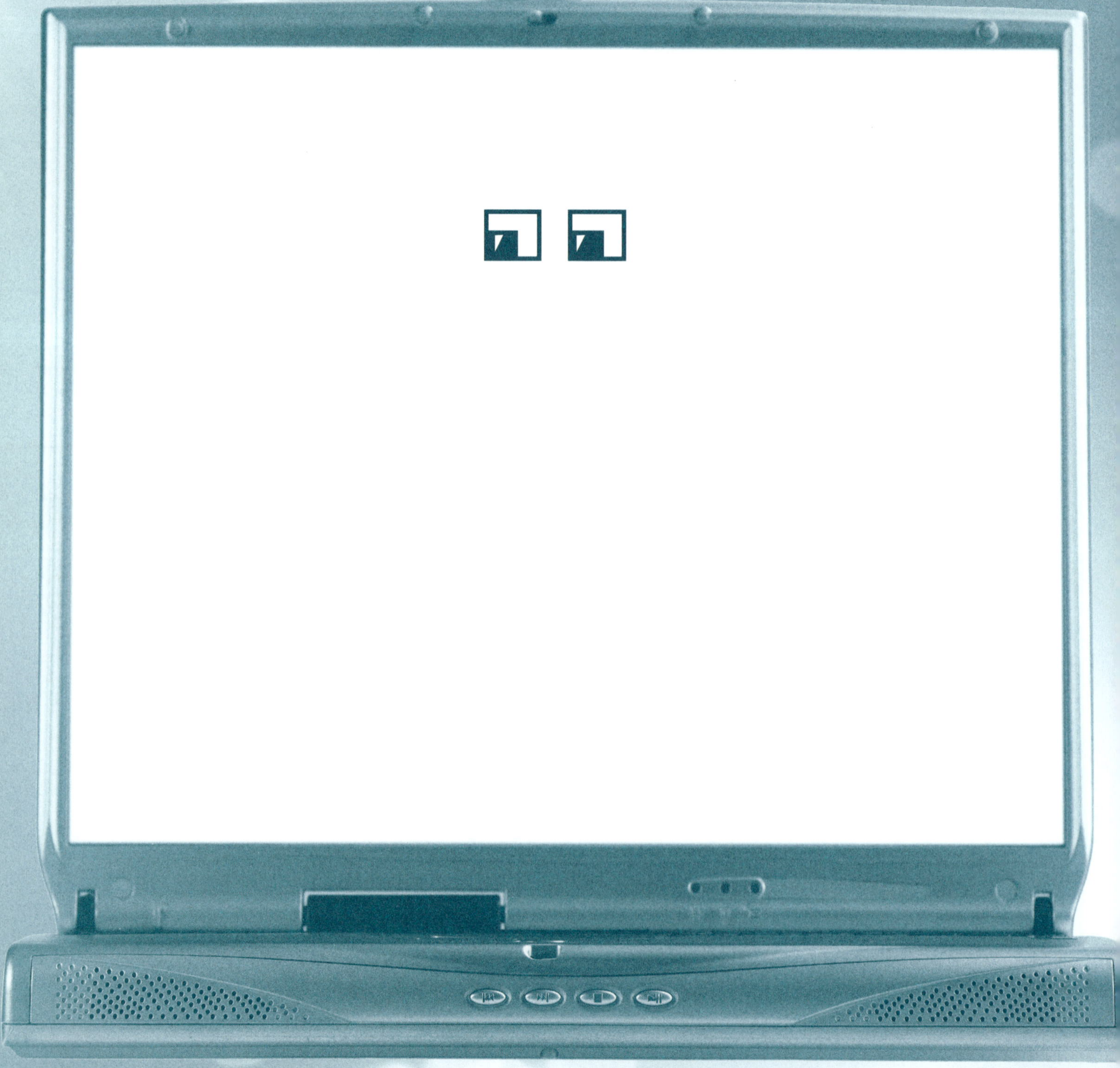

MANY ARTISTS, ILLUSTRATORS AND DESIGNERS USE COMPUTERS TO CREATE PICTURES OR EVEN ARTWORKS USING VIDEO OR SOUND.

Ancient art
Draw in the other half of this Greek vase.

COLOUR THE
VASE BLACK
AND THE LYRE
PLAYER IN
ORANGE, JUST
LIKE THE ANCIENT
GREEKS DID.

spot the difference!

Van Gogh painted this picture
of his Bedroom in Arles ...

... but this art forgery has ten mistakes!

Can you circle all ten differences?

FAKE

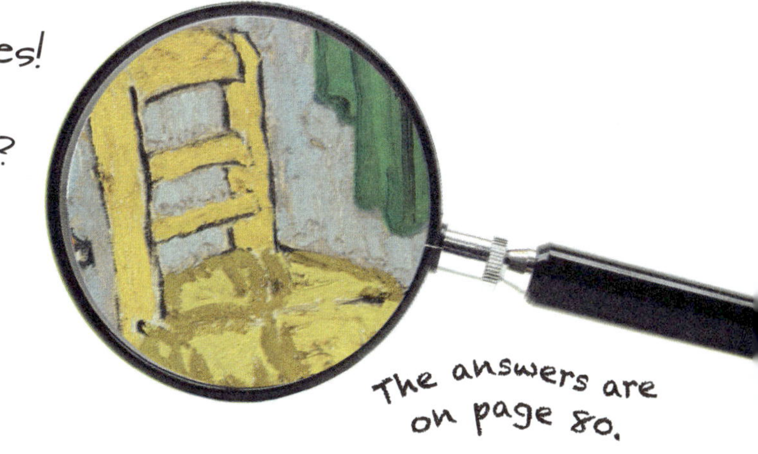

The answers are on page 80.

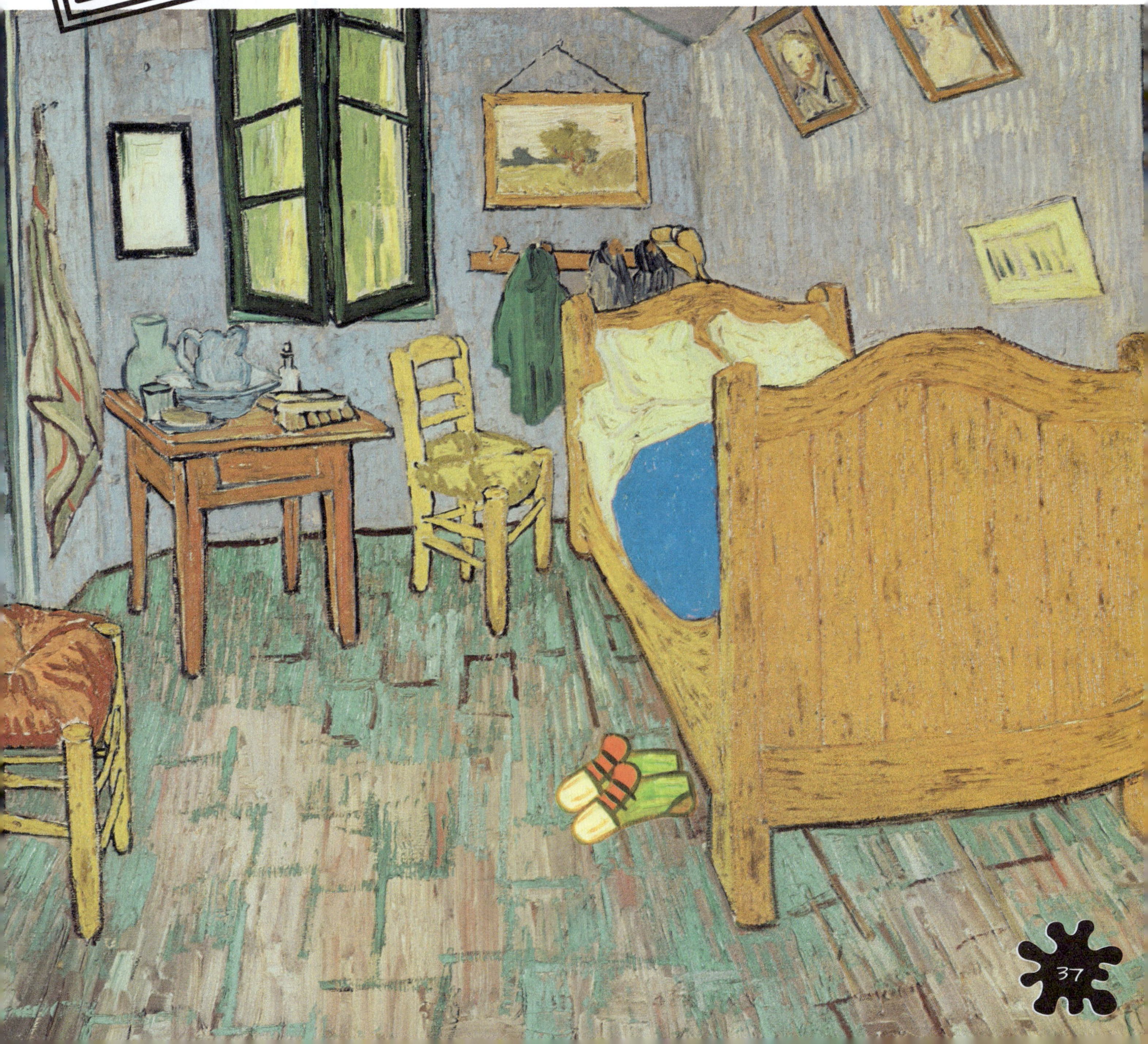

copy cat!

Artists often copy a small sketch onto a large canvas using a grid of squares. They call this 'squaring up'.

Copy the cat into the frame above.
Try drawing in one square at a time.

Children's Games

Bruegel painted many busy scenes filled with people.

PIETER BRUEGEL THE ELDER 1525 - 1569
FLEMISH PAINTER

40

Spot these games in Bruegel's Children's Games painting.

The answers are on page 80.

Go colour crazy!

Finish colouring in Paul Klee's Castle and Sun picture.

Fill the numbered shapes with their matching colours.

1 2 3 4 5 6 7 8

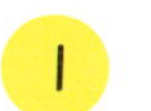

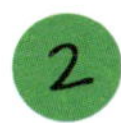

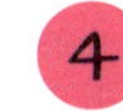

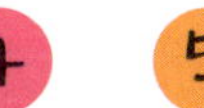

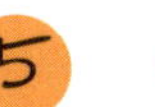

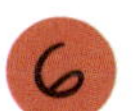

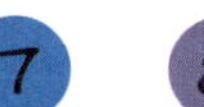

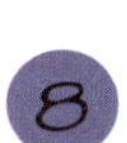

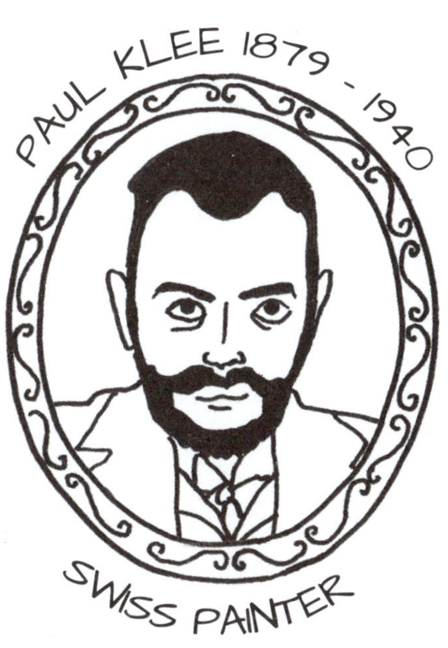

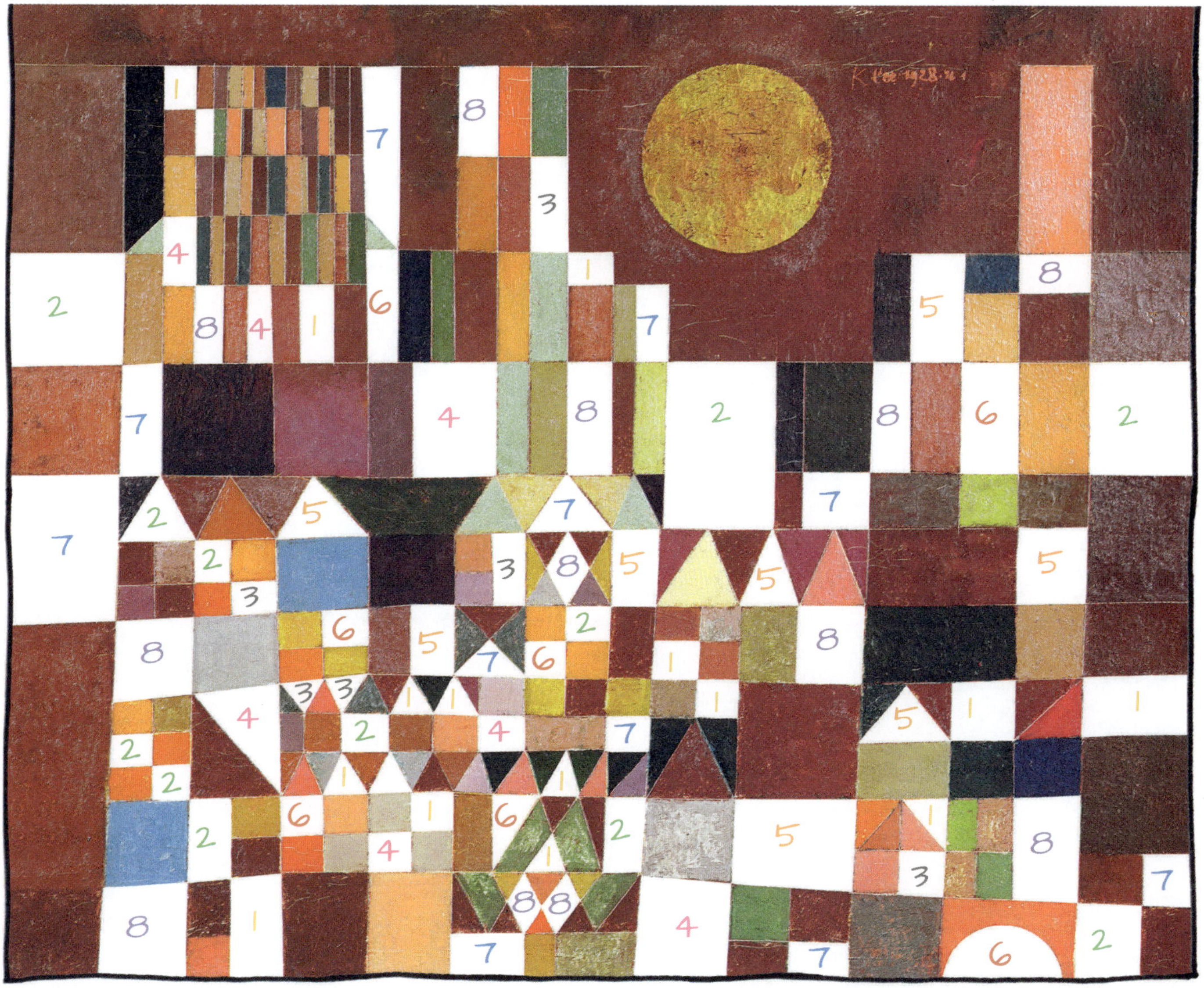

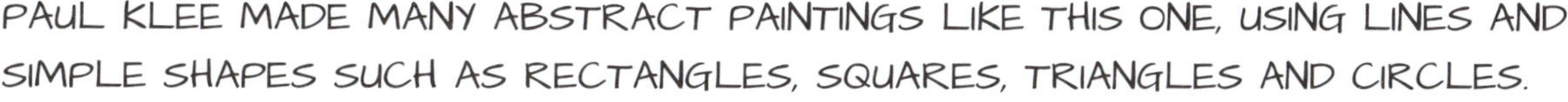

PAUL KLEE MADE MANY ABSTRACT PAINTINGS LIKE THIS ONE, USING LINES AND SIMPLE SHAPES SUCH AS RECTANGLES, SQUARES, TRIANGLES AND CIRCLES.

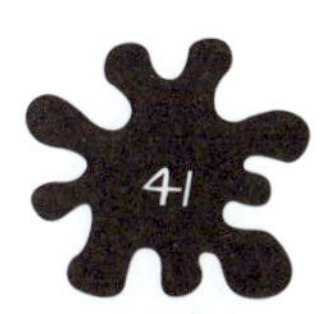

My art style!

Fill a notice board with things to inspire you.

Draw in your favourite things. You could stick in pictures cut out from magazines too.

My favourite word

My favourite animal

My favourite artist

My favourite pattern

My favourite colour

My favourite person

My favourite weather

My favourite shape

seasonal scenes
Have fun completing these pictures.

Make one scene warm and sunny and the other cold and snowy.

Summer

Winter

Patchwork patterns!
This traditional American quilt pattern is called tumbling blocks.
Finish colouring in the 3D pattern on the patchwork quilt below!
44

Just imagine ...

Play this great artistic memory game.

Artists can draw whatever they can imagine. Look at these pictures for one minute.

Then turn over the page and draw as many things as you can remember.

45

When you've finished, turn back over and see how many you got right.

A dotty portrait

Join the dots to reveal why this artist is so nervous.

HENRY VIII DECIDED TO MARRY
ANNE OF CLEVES AFTER SEEING
HER PORTRAIT, PAINTED BY THE
GERMAN ARTIST HANS HOLBEIN.
SHE WASN'T AS PRETTY AS HER
PICTURE, SO HENRY WAS ANGRY!

The answer is on page 80.

The Tree of Life
Klimt used patterns, bright colours and even gold in his paintings!
GUSTAV KLIMT 1862 - 1918
AUSTRIAN PAINTER
Finish the tree with more spirals, shapes and stickers.
Try these!
48

Monet's maze
Help Francis fish get to Art School.
Avoid the hungry pikes!
MONET LOVED PAINTING WATER AND FLOWERS, SO HE
BUILT A LILY POND WITH A CHINESE BRIDGE IN HIS GARDEN.
CLAUDE MONET 1840 - 1926
FRENCH PAINTER
START
FINISH!
The answer is on page 80.
49

Cave painting

Cave painters used natural materials, such as charcoal.

BANKSY, THE GRAFFITI ARTIST, ONCE SNEAKED A JOKE CAVE PAINTING ONTO THE WALLS OF THE BRITISH MUSEUM!

Draw some animals in the style of cave painters. You could use a black crayon or a felt-tipped pen.

Pretty papercuts

Fold and snip to make a beautiful butterfly!

1 CUT out this page. FOLD along these dotted lines.

2 Ask a grown-up to help you to CUT along the dashed line.

3 Fold along the dotted line in the middle of your cutout.

4 Snip out the little shapes. Ask a grown-up if it's too fiddly.

Stick your colourful butterfly on your bedroom window!

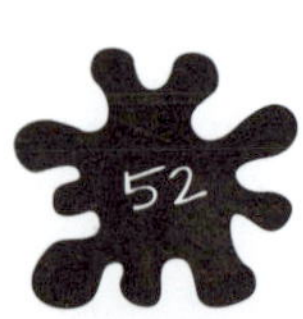

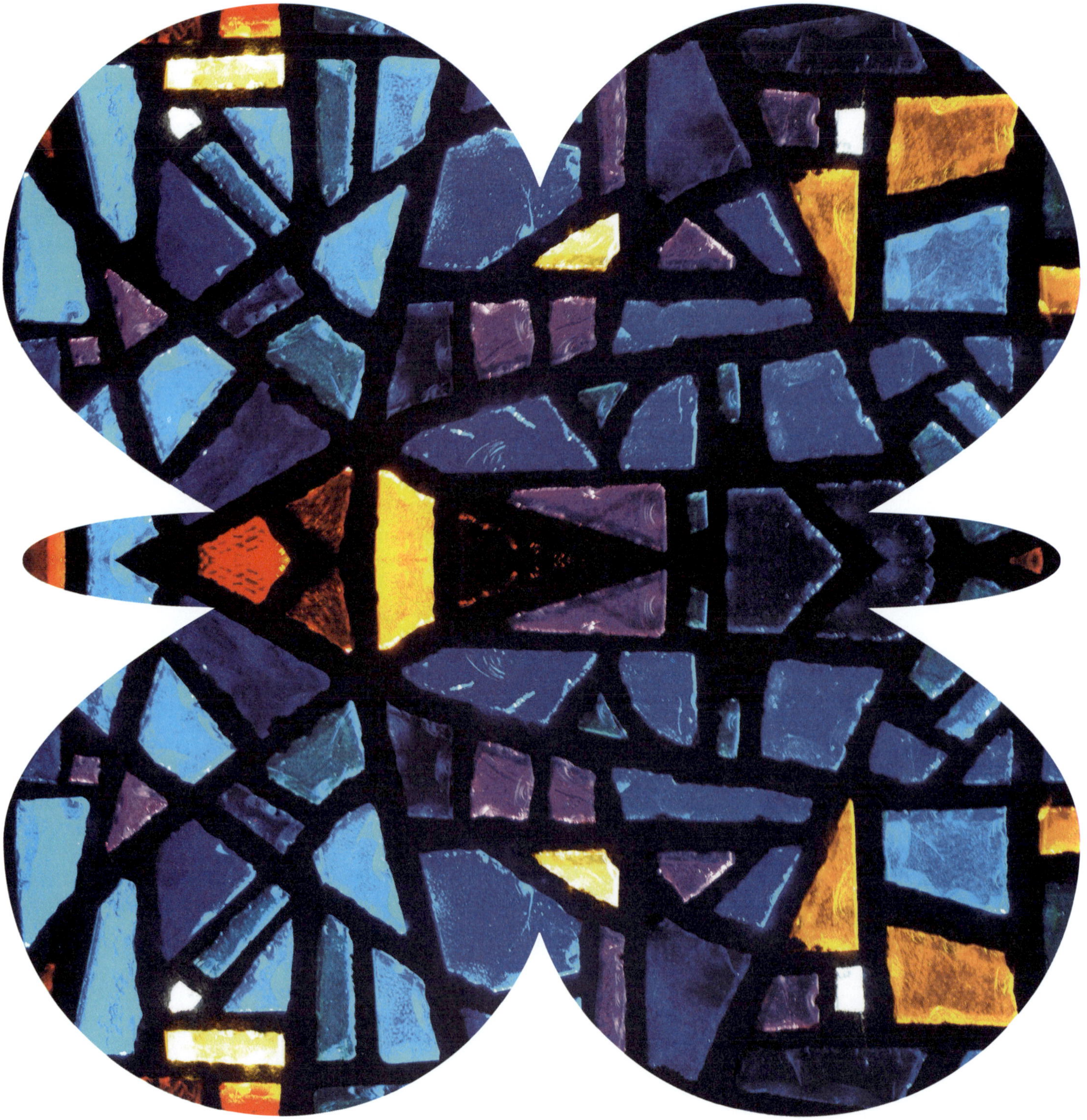

Arty door hangers

Arty door hangers

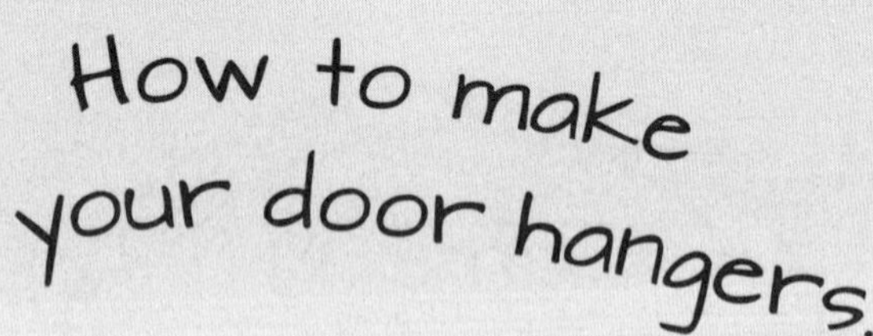

How to make
your door hangers.

1 Ask a grown-up
to help you CUT
OUT the two door
hanger shapes.

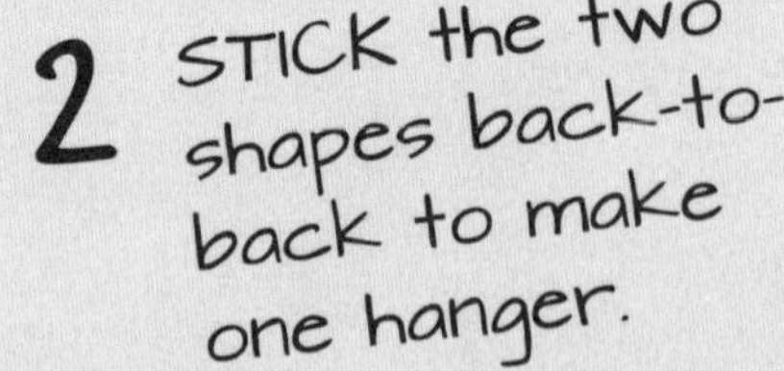

2 STICK the two
shapes back-to-
back to make
one hanger.

3 HANG it on your
bedroom door,
showing whichever
side you want!

Talking pictures

What are these pictures saying to each other?

MONA LISA
LEONARDO DA VINCI

SELF-PORTRAIT
ANDY WARHOL

SELF PORTRAIT IN
FRONT OF EASEL

VINCENT VAN GOGH

GIRL WITH A
PEARL EARRING

JOHANNES VERMEER

Making waves!

Hiroshige made water swirl by using different-shaped lines!

Can you spot these wave patterns in the picture?

1

2

3

4

Stormy sea at Naruto Rapids

The answers are on page 80.

Draw swirls, curves and lines to
create waves in a stormy sea!

Give your sea picture a stormy title.

painted patterns
Islamic artists create
wonderful geometric patterns.

Colour each shape
a different colour.
You can use circle
stickers too.

Extra art paper
Use this arty paper to decorate something you like!
Turn over
to check
out your
art paper.

A marvellous mask

Pablo Picasso, Henri Matisse and Amedeo Modigliani, three famous modern artists, were inspired by masks.

Turn over to find out how to make your mask.

How to make your mask

sticker fun!

Cool things to do with your stickers.

1 PLAY with your stickers over and over again on the STICKER SCENES at the end of the book and finish the MOSAIC STICKER PUZZLE on the following page!

2 Look out for these other pages where you can STICK your stickers:

- Finishing touches - page 4
- Collage castle - page 15
- A picnic picture - page 32
- My art style - page 42
- The **Tree of Life** - page 48
- Sticker quiz - page 68
- Art auction - page 76

Mosaic sticker puzzle
Romans decorated their floors with
mosaics made of tiny coloured stones.
Find the stickers
to finish this mosaic!
The answers are on page 80.
64

Fingerprint doodles

Get doodling to bring this scene to life.

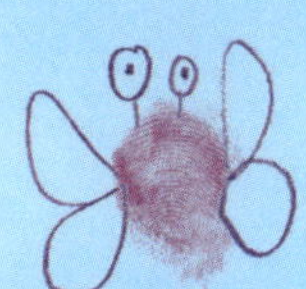

Add some doodles to these fingerprints to turn them into birds or fun creepy crawlies!

Add eyes and lots of legs to make a caterpillar!

65

A silly statue
Join the dots to see what's funny about the new statue!
MANY FAMOUS PEOPLE, INCLUDING THE RUSSIAN KING PETER THE GREAT, ARE CELEBRATED WITH HUGE PUBLIC STATUES.
The answer is on page 80.
66

puppet puzzle

Indonesian puppets are used to cast shadows onto a screen to create a shadow play.

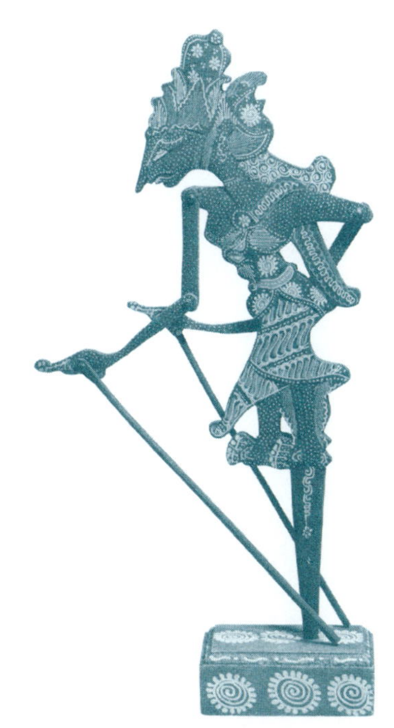

Which two puppet shadows are EXACTLY the same?

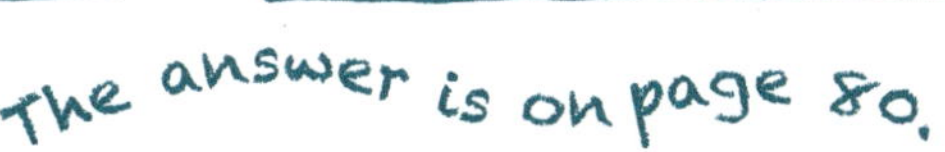
The answer is on page 80.

67

sticker quiz

A rainbow has seven colours - red, orange, yellow, green, blue, indigo and violet.

1. 🟡 + 🔵 = 🟢

2. ? + 🔴 = 🟣

3. 🔴 + ⚪ = ?

4. 🟡 + ? = 🟠

5. ? + ⚫ = ⬤

Use your paint splat stickers to solve this colour quiz!

The answers are on page 80.

Sunflowers
For Van Gogh yellow was the colour of joy.
VINCENT VAN GOGH 1853 - 1890
DUTCH PAINTER
Use different shades of yellow to colour these sunflowers.
69

Dalí's dream
Dreams gave Salvador Dalí ideas for paintings. What is he dreaming here?
SALVADOR DALÍ 1904 - 1989
SPANISH PAINTER
DALÍ'S MOST FAMOUS DREAM-LIKE PAINTING, THE PERSISTENCE OF MEMORY, SHOWS WATCHES MELTING ON A BEACH!
Z Z
Z Z
70

ARTIST MATCH UP GAME!

Match up some of the world's most famous artists in this fun card game.

Turn over to find out how to play. →

HOW TO PLAY

1. This game is for two to three players.
2. Get a grown-up to help you cut out all the game cards.
3. Mix up the cards and lay them all face down on a table.
4. Each player takes it in turn to flip over two cards. if they match up the player wins the cards and has another go.
5. If the two cards don't match you must turn them back over. Try to remember where they are for next go!
6. The game ends when the last two cards have been matched up. The winner is the player with the most artists. (It could be a draw!)

Frida Kahlo
Auguste Rodin
Edvard Munch
Albrecht Dürer
Mexican painter
French sculptor
Norwegian painter
German artist
Paul Klee
Gustav Klimt
Andy Warhol
Wassily Kandinsky
Swiss painter
Austrian painter
American artist
Russian painter
Ando Hiroshige
Salvador Dalí
Jackson Pollock
Paul Cézanne
Japanese artist
Spanish painter
American painter
French painter

An amazing abstract

Kandinsky used shapes, lines and colours to paint his feelings rather than things.

use your geometric-shaped stencils and stickers to create a picture.

Art auction
Paintings and other works of art are often sold at auctions.

Use your colouring pens, stencils and stickers here!

76

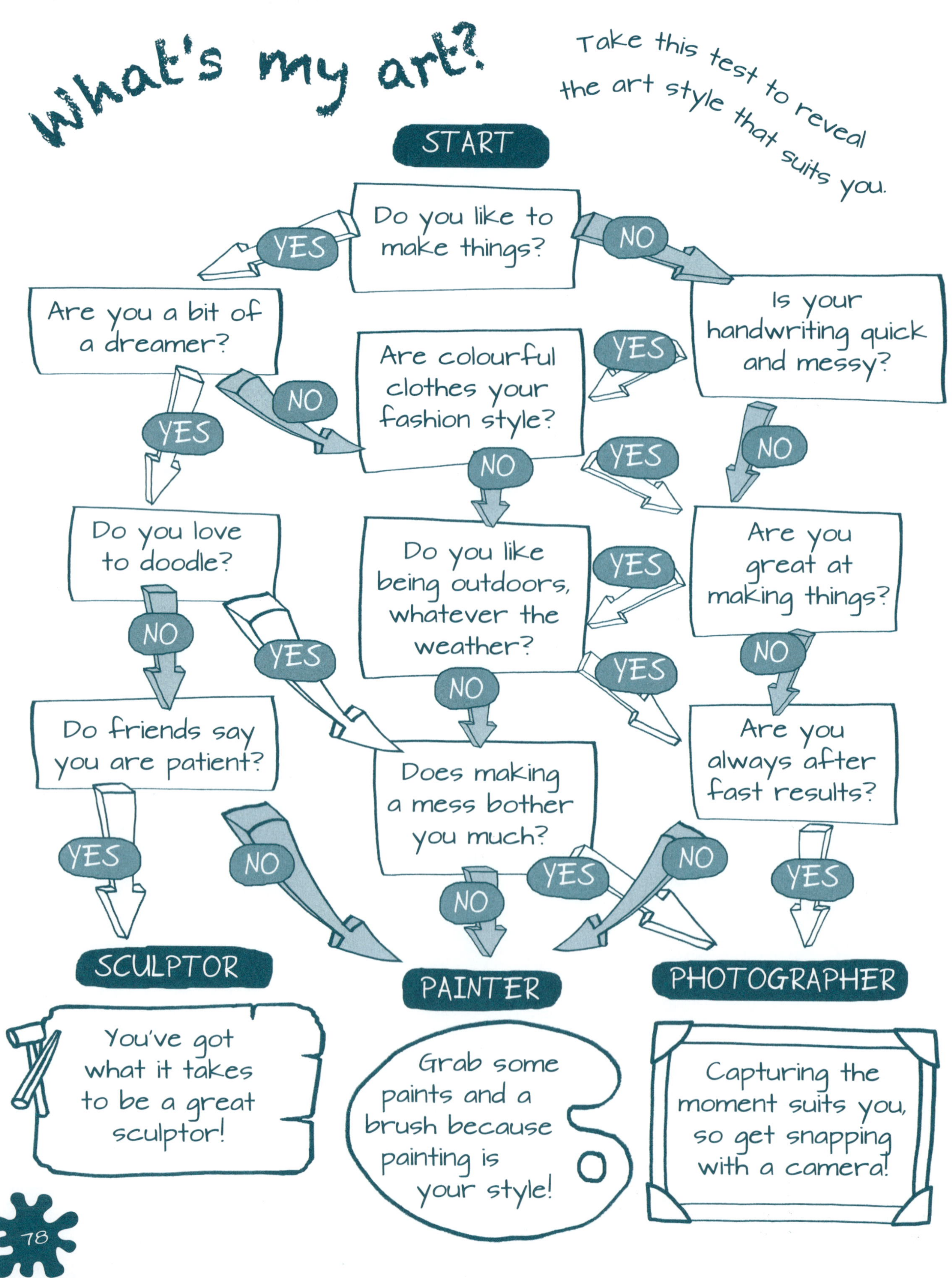

What's my art?
Take this test to reveal the art style that suits you.
START
Do you like to make things?
YES
NO
Are you a bit of a dreamer?
Are colourful clothes your fashion style?
YES
Is your handwriting quick and messy?
NO
YES
NO
YES
Do you love to doodle?
Do you like being outdoors, whatever the weather?
YES
Are you great at making things?
NO
YES
YES
NO
Do friends say you are patient?
Does making a mess bother you much?
Are you always after fast results?
YES
NO
NO
YES
NO
YES
SCULPTOR
PAINTER
PHOTOGRAPHER
You've got what it takes to be a great sculptor!
Grab some paints and a brush because painting is your style!
Capturing the moment suits you, so get snapping with a camera!
78

Your amazing artistic achievements deserve an official art award!

Fill in, cut out and hang on your wall.

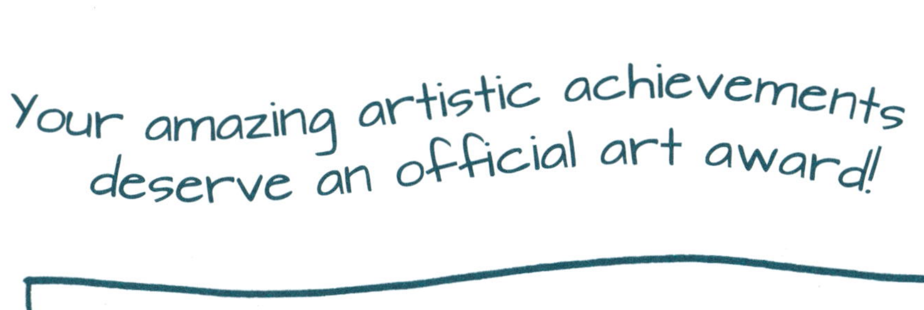

The Academy of Awesome Artists

We are delighted to award this certificate to

____

for being such an AMAZING ARTIST!

By order of

Ivor Paintbrush

____

Answers

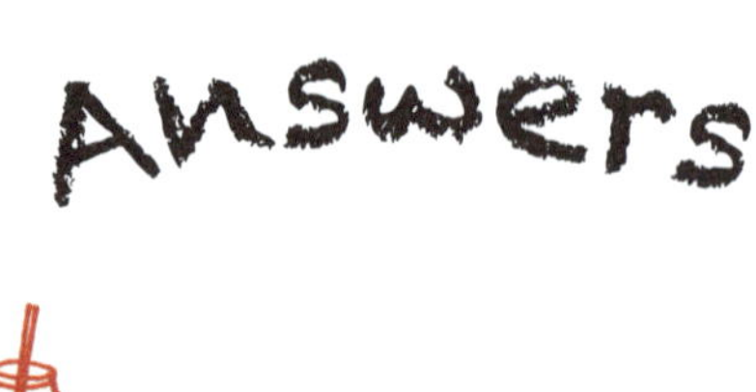